WALKING WITH GOD
THROUGH THE 12 STEPS

What I Learned about Honesty, Healing, Reconciliation and Wholeness

Frances Jay

LITURGY
TRAINING
PUBLICATIONS

Walking with God through the Twelve Steps
What I Learned about Honesty, Healing,
Reconciliation and Wholeness
by Frances Jay

Edited by David Fortier and
  Gregory F. Augustine Pierce
Cover Design by Tom A. Wright
Typesetting by Garrison Publications

Visit our website at www.ltp.org.

Originally published by ACTA Publications,
Chicago, Illinois.

Library of Congress Cataloging-in-Publication Data

Jay, Frances.
    Walking with God through the 12 Steps: what I learned
about honesty, healing, reconcilation, and wholeness/
Frances Jay.
          p.   cm.
    Originally published: Chicago: ACTA Publications, c1996
    ISBN: 1-56854-285-2
    1. Jay, Frances. 2. Christian biography—United States.
3. Alcoholics—United States—Biography. 4. Twelve-step
programs—Religious aspects—Christianity. I. Title.
BR1725.J383A3   1999
248.8' 629—dc21   9819808
                                                      CIP

Printed in the United States of America.

04 03 02 01 00   7 6 5 4 3

Contents . . .

Dedication

To my late husband, Frank, who loved me through it all and who still teaches me the true meaning of dying and rising to new life.

To the greatest gifts in my life—my children, children-in-law and grand-children.

To Barbara and my sister, Natalie, for being who you are.

To AA and all my companions who walked the journey before, with and after me.

To God, who loves me still.

Introduction . . .

What I had when I came to Alcoholics Anonymous was bad news . . . I couldn't stop drinking. What I received as gift was good news . . . I did stop.

What I had when I came to AA were two choices . . . death or insanity. What I received as gift was a third possibility . . . recovery.

What I had when I came to AA was the "what was" and the "what is." What I received as gift was the "what could be."

I came with a whole life that was unmanageable. The gift I received was "just one day."

I came with everything I had, which turned out to be nothing. Out of the nothingness, I saw a human being take shape.

The gifts were not handed to me all at once as I walked in the door of my first AA meeting. What was given to me was the promise that they would be found if I walked the path of the Twelve Steps. Now I try to carry the message to others. What is the message? I am . . . I am an alcoholic who has not had a drink today. This is possible.

Years ago, I pictured myself as a young, responsible, Scripture-reading, church-going, God-fearing wife and mother. I was good. Life was good, even with the snags that kept it from being easy. With all this strength and goodness in place, I slowly and unintentionally followed the path to alcoholism.

Then I was strong and determined to do good, yet completely ineffective in overcoming evil. I succumbed to the power of alcohol and denied that it was a weakness. The increasingly noticeable contradiction between my "good" self-image and the reality of the "evil" person I was becoming gnawed at me constantly, but I kept getting around it by blaming others for the evil and by comforting myself as the helpless victim.

The journey of conversion, of changing my thinking about God, myself and others has not been painless, but I no longer try to avoid pain. I don't go looking for it, but when it comes I don't run away, because I now believe pain is the door to wholeness.

Part of my journey is the move from shame and blame to a real desire for honesty, healing, reconciliation and wholeness.

As an aside, although I began to reform my life because of alcoholism, what I have discovered covers the human condition. The thoughts on the following pages are not limited to alcoholism but are about life itself.

Also, I have been intrigued with the stories of Scripture from an early age and can better see myself in their context since making contact with the AA program.

For me, the Twelve Steps of AA capture the essence of the scriptural message in a way that I can follow, and as I live each new day the stories continue to provide a new understanding of God, myself and others.

Throughout my journey, there has been growth toward fulfillment.

Sometimes I am aware of this growth like the budding leaves on the tree.

Sometimes it is hidden deep within, like the life-giving sap that nourishes and sustains through the cold, bleak times of life.

The seeds were planted, then watered and cared for by those who have come to love life. But only God gives the growth.

We have no power over the seeds except to surrender them to the earth and let God raise them up. He will do so . . . in due season.

In Due Season . . .

I saw you when you first came, O great tree, with
    rope-like roots,
        a clump of earth and
            burlap bag for feet.
Your new home a water-filled hole
    between my house and the street.

With no leaves on the skinny branches
    and a trunk about two inches or so,
        you still showed signs of being alive.
No way to know what was happening inside of you.
    Will you make it? Will you survive?
    No way to know.

Soon, your posture changed and you began to lean.
    Perhaps the rain had washed away your foothold
    Or you were pushed too hard by a wind unseen.
One who cared very much for you knew what you needed;
    A sturdy metal stake
        and strong thin wire
    Pulled you back and freed you to grow higher.

Then winter came with longer nights and shorter days;
    less warmth from the sun's rays.
        Not only would the bitter winds blow;
        You would know
        The tingling numbness of frost and ice and snow.

You were so young, so weak, so inexperienced
    in living the life of a tree!
        I wanted to surround you with warmth,
          protect you from rejection,
            spare you pain;
    The same comforts I wanted for me.

The one who cared for you spoke through
    an understanding smile at my concern.

Growth includes many trials, many pains,
    That's how we learn
        what we will become.
A hidden strength you cannot see,
        the sap—the life blood—will run free
        and fill the heart down to the roots
            To nourish and sustain this tree.

Trust me for truly I have come to know
    a Power whispers deep within
        of stronger roots
            and thicker bark,
        of fragile buds that bear the mark
            of small green leaves
    urging "grow, lovely one, grow."

Truth had been spoken. The Power was there.
Today, birds nest in your leafy hair
    And squirrels find a playground where
        once your empty arms held little life.
You have answered your Creator's call
        to change and grow and live through all
            the seasons of life, O great tree!

I have seen you small and new,
    full and green,
        crowned in royal gold and then
    barren, humbled, glory unseen
        you turned inward once again
            to find reality and truth
    and so you grew.

With joy I thank you, O great tree,
    for waiting and hoping,
        for struggling and coping,
            for dying and rising
For being God's servant and teaching me
    to sing the Alleluia of new life
        . . . all in due season.

It started many years ago. My husband and I were sitting in the living room watching TV. Our four young children were already in bed. I was not feeling well when I came home from work that day, but I thought I would improve if I just relaxed for the rest of the evening. After an hour or so, my complaints drove my husband to call the doctor. When the doctor heard my symptoms, he concluded that I might be having an allergic reaction and that my blood vessels were constricted, producing the coldness, faintness and anxiety that I was experiencing. He prescribed a straight shot of whiskey to dilate the blood vessels. It worked. I went to bed and slept quite peacefully. This same scene was played out several times over the next few months. No need to call the doctor; I knew what would help. What I did not realize was that I was subconsciously making a connection between physical discomfort, anxiety, sleeplessness and the relief provided by alcohol.

How easy it became over the next years to choose alcohol as a solution to all other problems that arose. When I had had a rough day at work, alcohol would relax me. When there wasn't enough money to pay the bills, alcohol would remove the concern from my mind. When my husband and I no longer seemed to be happy with each other, alcohol would extract me from the relationship. If I could just get a good night's sleep, I could handle the next day. It was so subtle and non-threatening, and at no time did I feel that I was doing anything wrong.

It was several years before I realized that both

drinking and not drinking produced the same symptoms of physical discomfort, anxiety and sleeplessness. I began to wake up several hours after going to sleep terribly nauseated and would have to spend a long time in the bathroom trying to empty my stomach. When I would return to bed, I would be restless and unable to go back to sleep. So I would fix myself a drink and, more often than not, repeat the whole episode.

At some point, my system apparently adjusted to the abuse of alcohol and no longer rebelled with the nausea and vomiting. Then came the sweats and chills and pounding heartbeat. I no longer felt "refreshed" in the morning, even though I had not had a drink for five or six hours. I still did not drink during the day because I had to work, though sometimes the residual effects of the "night before" made me feel very "green around the edges."

I would go home and dutifully perform my wifely and motherly chores such as cooking supper, doing laundry, helping the children with homework and sending them to bed. Then I would crash! Fortunately for the children, they got older and as time went on were able to fend for themselves. Unfortunately for me, this helped me develop more feelings of being unwanted and more time to start drinking earlier. I felt alone and sad and miserable, but I could not stop drinking. It was no longer a choice. I was hooked.

Looking back on my own experience, it is easier for me to relate to "the fall" of Adam and Eve. A fall implies dropping from a higher to a lower level, and we had all three accomplished that. The question put to them by the serpent—whether God told them not to eat from any of the trees—was intended to trigger their awareness of their limitations. They defended their position that they were not limited in *all* ways, but only in *one* way—they couldn't eat from the tree of knowledge of good and evil. Even with only one limitation, however, they obviously weren't in control. Someone else was greater than they were. Now they were vulnerable to pride—the temptation not to be limited at all.

My story wasn't much different. As I became more and more conscious of the limitations in my life, I tried harder and harder to gain control of myself, other people and reality.

Did I ever recognize the "serpent" I was listening to and following? Was I aware that I was choosing a "lower" form of living? Did I realize when it was happening that I was being led away from God, my true self and the others who were part of my life?

No. Just like Adam and Eve, I allowed myself to be deceived.

Now that I am sober, however, another story from Genesis is a daily occurrence: The earth, sea, sky, sun, moon, animals are all in place each day when I wake up. Many times I am still tempted by values other than those set forth by my "Higher Power," and sometimes I still fall for the illusions rather than the reality. But at least now I don't fall for the illusion that alcohol is my friend. It is my enemy and I know it. Each day, I am given the freedom to be all that a human can be, but I cannot be God. That one restriction no longer disturbs me. It has become instead a motivating factor in my journey to become fully human. The focus is now on what I can be, not what I can't be.

Now, I ask myself questions like these: Do I stay with the values of the one who gave birth to me, or do I try out new values? Are some values right and others wrong, or are they just different? Is one way better than the other, or can they both be good?

In spite of the tension brought about by these questions, they are a necessary process for maturing and becoming a person. Mistakes will be made. I have the potential to both hurt and help myself and others through my choices.

Sometimes I can check out the consequences ahead of time by looking at another's experience, but many times I will learn the hard way — by trial and error. I have to make judgments based on the information that is available to me, and sometimes the information is incomplete or erroneous.

From the beginning, the information I was working with—that alcohol was helpful and freeing—was both incomplete and erroneous. Discernment—the ability to see what is obscure or concealed—was missing. Not taking the time to get more information and exercise discernment was what allowed me to think drinking, escape from reality and blaming others were good things. But how many people I know went to AA first to get the facts about drinking before they started doing it? None.

Such choosing without being able to see the outcome is my experience of "eating of the tree of the knowledge of good and evil." I came to know them both, but I guess I was assuming it would be quite clear which was which. What really happened was that I could no longer tell one from the other.

As a child, I was told that evil was a fallen angel now restricted to being a serpent, but I didn't see any snakes in my glass of booze! Now I don't even try to guess what evil might look like. I know evil is deceptive, and I know I can be deceived.

That is why I need the discernment of the larger group of AA members to help me identify some of the disguises that evil wears. AA also helps me find the good—which is often hidden but never disguised. I need both of these elements in my life today. Just avoiding evil or drinking is not enough. I need to find truth and sobriety.

Who will roll the stone away?

(MK 16:3)

Step One

We admitted we were powerless over alcohol — that our lives had become unmanageable.

I knew I had a problem. I even knew what the problem was — drinking too much. I just didn't know how to get out from under it alone. I had desperately tried to stop many times, and I could do it for a few days. But I couldn't stay stopped.

One night while sitting at the kitchen table (*drinking*) trying to read the neighborhood newspaper (*it is important to try to look like you're doing something other than what you're really doing*) through slightly unfocused eyes, I came across an article about the opening of an alcoholism treatment ward in a nearby hospital. Here was an answer to a prayer I hadn't even prayed yet.

I wasn't sure what the exact definition of an "alcoholic" was, so the word didn't bother me. I just knew it had something to do with drinking too much, and I had already told myself that was my problem.

The next day, I called for an appointment. The day after that, I went for an interview. I took a 20-question test and probably lied on half of the answers. I didn't want to look bad!

The intake counselor and I talked about many of the different "symptoms" of alcoholism — not just drinking too much. As she kept talking about the characteristic behavior of an "alcoholic," the word started to bother me a whole lot. I didn't have all those defects. I just drank too much. How quickly admission goes out the window and denial flies in!

But things were bad for me. I was on the verge of despair. Perhaps it was because I was becoming more and more aware of the difference between what I used to be and what I had become.

I used to be an intelligent and responsible person. Now I wasn't even smart enough to figure out how to stop doing what was destroying my life.

I used to have respect for myself and concern about the example I set for others. Now, here I was remembering that just last week, in the dead of winter, I walked out my front door wearing my nightgown and my husband's galoshes to go to the corner store to buy a bottle of booze.

I used to be a mother who took delight in caring for my children, and now I couldn't be sure if I could get out of bed in the morning, let alone get them dressed and off to school.

I used to be a choir member and organist at church, and now I just dragged myself there on Sunday because I was too afraid not to go.

I used to be a Den Mother in Cub Scouts, a Brownie and Girl Scout leader, and gave workshops for the Scout District, city-wide, to help train others for those roles. Now I could hardly find my way to my own bathroom, let alone lead anyone else in anything.

I used to enjoy my family and friends, and now I didn't even want them to see me. I used to be free to do many things, and now I was enslaved to drinking.

I told the counselor I was willing to be whatever I had to be to get help. I would be an alcoholic. She informed me I would be in a locked ward for 30 days, except to attend AA meetings three nights a week, and could possibly get a weekend pass to go home after three weeks.

Now here I was in one of those situations where I have to make a choice based on the available information. My mind was going crazy trying to decide between the pain and degradation of staying and explaining my prolonged absence from home and the thought of going back home with no relief from my desperate situation, which I could not change on my own. Which would be worse, I wondered, subjecting myself to *them* or to *me*?

(Notice I didn't give any thought to which choice would be the better one. I only chose which would be the worse. I decided to take my chances with *them*.)

When the hospital accepted me as a patient, I had, in so many words, confirmed that what I had been willing to "admit" in theory was really true, and I resented it immediately. For me it was more than just admitting I was an "alcoholic," it was admitting that I was doing something wrong . . . and that someone else knew how to do it right.

On those occasions when I had tried to stop drinking but couldn't stay stopped, it was because I always had access to some booze. In a locked alcoholism treatment ward, there is no access to booze, and you stay stopped.

Those who had serious physical problems from the withdrawal were kept in their rooms under medical observation and care for a few days. The rest of us had to participate in the scheduled programs. There were those other "alcoholics" to get acquainted with, educational seminars to attend, weekly sessions with the hospital chaplain, and AA meetings three nights a week.

My expectations weren't very high, but my misery level was, so I decided to try to be more open to this new experience. I found some other people in the program who seemed to be in the same boat as I, and that made participating a little easier. At least I was not the only one who had fallen from grace, had a drinking problem, felt such shame and hurt this much. (I think I understood then why Eve wanted to be sure Adam joined her in eating the apple!)

I soon learned that I was in an environment where there was safety in shared weakness while we were finding shared strength. I have to admit that this is one of the things I often found lacking in the "church people" I had attempted to confide in. There didn't seem to be any sinners among them, and I felt uncomfortable and out-of-place. They were good at diagnosing what was wrong with me, but not very good at admitting they had any shortcomings.

Filled with my previous experiences, that "shame and blame" was everyone's answer to wrongdoing, I expected that I was going to be held up as an example of what *not* to do or be. That did not happen here. Shame and blame were *not* the main thrust. What were they after then?

I attended my first AA meeting "on the evening of the first day." What I remember most vividly was my astonishment at the number of people who were at the meeting. There were far more of us with this problem than I had suspected. I found the numbers encouraging, not because there were so many but because here was a sanctuary where people could die and rise, admit there was a problem and do something about it—together. This insight was what gave me the courage to continue on.

When the dozen or so of us patients entered the meeting room, we were warmly greeted by those who were already there. They were actually glad to see us — not because it would make for a bigger, better meeting or add to their numbers, but because they knew we had taken a step in the direction of recovery and could finally find help for ourselves.

The meeting began and the chairperson welcomed everyone, specifically mentioning "all those from the rehab unit."

Oh, my God! They've noticed us. Is there anyone here who might recognize me? My eyes quickly shot around the room. Nobody I knew.

The chairperson proceeded by saying, "There are three choices for the alcoholic: death, insanity or recovery. We welcome you to this meeting where we offer a program of recovery."

If I do not remember anything else I heard at that meeting, I remember that statement. Death, insanity or recovery. They were—and remain—my three choices.

"How It Works" and the "Thought for the Day" were read by members and a topic was suggested. People began their comments by saying their first name, saying they were recovering alcoholics, some even saying they were "grateful" alcoholics.

Grateful, recovering alcoholic! I have since spoken those words a thousand times, but I was certainly not at that point that night.

Somebody talked about denial. When we are in denial, change is not possible because we either don't think change is necessary or we spend our time trying to fix the wrong things or the wrong people.

I'm here, aren't I? I gave my name and said I'm an alcoholic, didn't I? So why are we talking about denial?

I found out over many years of meetings that being an alcoholic isn't the only thing we're likely to have denied for a long time. We have denied that we are human. We have denied that we've been playing God. We've denied that we were wrong. Fortunately, there are eleven more steps that introduce us to these areas of denial.

What the Twelve Steps suggested I should do was not a problem; doing it was a different story. Though I had admitted I was an alcoholic, I had a hard time truly accepting it because my mind still wanted to think of it as a "bad" thing. Fixed in my "either/or" way of thinking, I naturally looked only at the "what is" (bad) or the "what can be" (good).

Later I learned to see both "what is" and "what can be" as the same person in different stages of growth. The Twelve Steps, the meetings, these people were an invitation for me to accept the "what is" and move toward the "what can be."

Participation would mean change, conversion, re-forming my whole life. It would entail giving up my old ideas, my old beliefs, my old habits and learning new ones. That was very frightening. It was like hanging in mid-air clinging to a big, fat rope that I had come to trust to support me and being invited to let go and grab a very thin thread. I grabbed the thread, but for quite some time I kept the other hand on the rope. I had to learn to trust the thread.

Reflection Questions

1. To what (or when) do you feel enslaved?

2. The alcoholic has three choices: death, insanity, or recovery. What are your choices?

3. What is the big, fat rope you cling to? What thread do you want to trust?

Blessed are those who have not seen and yet have come to believe.

(JN 20:29)

Step Two

Came to believe that a Power greater than ourselves could restore us to sanity.

$\mathcal{W}$hen my 30 days were up, I had to leave the safety and security of the rehab unit and go back out into the real world. On my one and only weekend pass, I had returned home to find everything just as I had left it, including my half-empty bottle of booze. I did not want to drink, but still felt terribly afraid of my weakness. So I prayed as I have never prayed before because I would no longer have the hospital to rely on.

I was going to have to make a personal decision about what I wanted for me—even in the presence of alcohol and my own weaknesses. I chose recovery and rejected death and insanity. I now know that what I reject will not disappear from my life. There will always be the same three options, and I must choose the one I want for me each day.

Since my thoughts, my beliefs, my previous choices, and yes, even the rehab unit, were all part of the big, fat rope I had been hanging on to, I knew I could not let go of it unless I had something else to cling to. I was going to have to trust the thread — the God I believed in but didn't really know. If God hadn't stopped me from falling before, would he stop me from falling now?

I was very tired and still carried a heavy burden; would this thin thread break under the weight?

Much later I became aware that my questions were prompted by my awareness of my own limitations and fears of failure. Like Moses, who offered his reasons why he was probably not the best candidate to lead his people out of slavery because of his lack of eloquence, I was checking out the possibility that I might not have what it takes to make it.

As I kept thinking about the thread, a little voice just kept saying, "I will be with you. Do not be afraid."

When I first grabbed onto the thread, I didn't feel any different and my life didn't seem any different, except that I had been able to stop drinking once again. But this time *was* different. I had made a choice to trust and believe in someone other than myself, even though I had no idea what the experience was going to be like. All I knew about the God I was trying to understand at that point was that he seemed willing to hang on to me. I did not fall, the thread did not break—though it got stretched pretty tight sometimes. My body had recovered from the effects of alcohol, but my thoughts and emotions had not really changed. So I went back to my family with pretty much the same reactions and responses I had before.

It didn't take long before I realized I was very anxious and desperate for help. I would cry over every little upset, and I wanted to blame my family for my misery. I locked myself in my room one night just to get away from them, but they kept knocking on my door and insisting that I come out. I didn't realize I was doing as I had always done—either try to change them or isolate myself from them. As I lay on the bed crying, I heard myself thinking, "Oh, God! What am I going to do? If I stay like this, I am either going to drink or go crazy!"

Again, I had another thought, "What about your other choice—recovery? Perhaps you could go to a meeting." I got up, grabbed $3.00 out of my purse

($2 for bus fare, $1 for the AA basket), flew out of the room and put on my coat.

My husband said, "Where are you going? You just got home from the hospital a few days ago. We haven't seen you for a month. Spend some time with us."

I opened the door and kept going. I had just learned something else about the God I was trying to understand. He could communicate with me. He could remind me of the path I had chosen and lead me on the way.

When I arrived at the meeting, I was anxious to talk about my experience but didn't know just what topic to suggest. Rather than look stupid, I kept quiet. The young man next to me said, "I have a topic. I'm not sure if can identify my problem, but I think it is an unmanageable life. How do I learn to live the life I really have with the people that are really in it without constant anxiety and frustration?"

Everyone shared their own experiences and what they had had to change about themselves. Mostly, it seemed to center on not blaming others for how we feel, changing our response to people, places and things rather than trying to control them, and not being afraid to ask for help when we need it.

The young man got the help he was looking for that night and so did I, but not because I was willing to take the risk of being human. I learned that another person can be strong enough to show me where I am weak. The God I am trying to understand can communicate with me and teach me both directly and through others.

I also came to believe that God could communicate to others through me. I was scheduled to be the speaker at a meeting at a halfway house where I knew many of the residents. They had been with me in rehab and had probably heard most of my story, but even so I knew it was important to tell it like it is. I prayed on the way to the meeting that those who heard me would be able to hear their Higher Power speaking to them and that he would be with them and lead them just as he had done for me.

I shared my "how it was, what happened and what it's like today," including my new-found relationship with a God who is so different from the one I had known before. I talked about the thin thread that I had learned to trust and how strong it really was. I told how instead of the condemnation and punishment I had been so afraid of, I found a Higher Power who only wanted to heal me and help me. I shared how, instead of remaining fixed in the shame and blame that had kept me imprisoned for so long, I too had learned to ask for help and healing.

When a speaker finishes his or her talk, it is customary to ask for comments from those present. Some had had similar experiences, some had not. Some were still struggling to believe in a Higher Power, and some were still denying that they needed to be restored to sanity.

There was one young man sitting directly opposite me at the end of the table. He had stared at me intently through the whole talk, and I couldn't help but be aware of it. When it was his turn to comment, all he said was, "I was planning to do something very foolish. I was going to leave here and end my life because I didn't think I could live without drinking. When you were talking, I know I heard God's voice and he was talking to me. He was telling me to hang on, and I'm going to try to do that. Thank you for sharing your story and your thread."

I was completely overwhelmed, awestruck at the young man's comment, because I was hearing God saying to me, "I did what you asked."

The tears were rolling down my cheeks then, and they still do now, when I think about this experience. The God I am coming to understand is willing to communicate to others through me. I continue to pray today for the willingness to let him do so.

The God I understand today is very different from the one I used to believe in. All I really had before were beliefs *about* God, second-hand experiences or the convictions of others.

I knew the Bible stories about the Exodus from slavery and how God had worked through Moses as his "visible" partner. I knew about the healing of the lepers, the crippled and the blind. I knew about the woman about to be stoned for adultery and how she was freed from the shame and blame of the mob. I also knew the images of God given to me by my parents, my teachers, the clergy and my fellow church-goers, plus the ones I had formed on my own.

First and foremost, I never had difficulty believing that there is a God. I have always been a Scripture-loving, church-going woman. I also had no difficulty believing that he was greater than me. My difficulty occurred in letting him restore me to sanity, because I had to let go of my old ideas of what was really real and what was merely a projection by me onto God and other people.

My head and lips professed God's power and authority, but I was really the one who had created the world I lived in and I was the one I trusted to take care of my life. I had convinced myself that the evil behind the pain in my life was outside of me and so the solution was to either recreate the world or isolate myself. I believed what I was doing was rational, and my belief allowed for optimism even when reality was trying to teach me otherwise.

For a while, I am sure I even believed that God approved of my actions or else he would have forcibly stopped me from destroying myself. Though I was completely unaware of it initially, my thoughts and actions were actually a rebellion against God for letting the world and humanity be the way they are. I had an unconscious belief that I could do it better. It was only after ten years of frustration, suffering and failure to bring about this better life that I was willing to admit defeat and powerlessness.

God had been well-defined in my mind and I presumed I knew what he would or would not do, what his "acceptable" behavior would be in given circumstances. Some of what I believed was true, but none of it was personal. It has only been since I have made my own exodus journey out of slavery that I have come to know the pillar of cloud who leads me by day and the pillar of fire who protects me at night (Ex 13:21-22).

It is only now that I see the divine and the human hand-in-hand on a journey together across the desert to the promised land. There have been joy and pain, nourishment and hunger, grumbling and thanksgiving, surrender and rebellion, springs of water and dry, hot sand. I have never really wanted to turn back, but there were times when I didn't want to move on. Then I'd know I had to break camp and catch up with the pillar of cloud. There is always the bronze serpent mounted on a pole (Nm 21:9) that I have to look upon so I will remember what poisoned me and nearly took my life, and I have to remember the other idols and false gods that I created so I can say "no" to them and "yes" to the God I now believe is real. I have learned that when God defines himself as "I AM" (Ex 3:14), I should stop there and not limit him to my current understanding.

God's revelation is ongoing, and I usually find it in the desert. The desert is the place where I'm out of the cultural do's and don'ts and away from the human attractions. There I can focus on my relationship with God—not on "outside" things but on "inside" things. The desert for me is not a bad place to be anymore. It is where I find myself each time I have been freed from a "captive power" and have safely eluded the forces that are trying to take me back. I now know where I have come from, but I still don't know how to get where I want to go. I need guidance and experiences that will help me choose the right path.

Yet the desert experience isn't about doing what other people think I should do. It's not even about doing what I think I should do. It's about freedom. Freedom to become whole. Freedom to learn about who God really is for me—not my human projections of who he is. Freedom to learn about who I am—not other human projections of who I am. God is God. I don't know what that means in its completeness, but what I know is enough for this day of the journey. I am still me—imperfect and human—but God seems to understand that, so there is comfort when I am afraid, guidance when I don't know which way to go, nourishment when I'm hungry, patience when I lag behind and encouragement to turn more and more of my life over to his care.

How do I know God does all of this? I hear it in my life through the Twelve Steps of AA, in the voices of my fellow travelers sharing their experiences on the journey of recovery. I see God's presence in the many miracles performed in the lives of people who were once enslaved, physically sick, emotionally crippled and spiritually dead.

I have come to believe that "he who has promised is faithful" (Heb 10:23).

Reflection Questions

1. Where are the places/areas you feel safe? What are the patterns in your life that are barriers to your physical and emotional well-being?

2. Are you in the habit of blaming others? What is the result?

3. Is the God you believe in today different from the God of your past?

Your Father knows what you need

(MT 6:8)

Step Three

Made a decision to turn our will and our lives over to the care of God <u>as we understood him</u>.

$\mathcal{M}$y sponsor put it to me very simply: "We are powerless over alcohol *and* over people, places and things."

"That covers everything!" I cried. "What am I in control of then?"

"Your own will," she said very softly, "and I think you'll find that to be about as much as you can handle."

She was right. My will is very strong, but not very powerful. Here's what I mean. I could make a decision not to withdraw from my family when they upset me, but later I'd find myself back in my room, crying and desperate. I could make a decision to attend at least three meetings a week, but then I'd stay home because it was raining too hard. I could make a decision to go out and look for a job, but I'd end up just reading the want ads for another month. All my reasons for *not* doing what I had decided to do seemed justifiable. In fact, my family supported me in some of what I was *not* doing. So did some of my friends.

Something inside of me kept gnawing away at my excuses, however, reminding me that I was getting back into the same old rut. I came to the same conclusion that St. Paul had arrived at: I do what I don't want to do and I don't do what I do want to do (Rom 7:15-19). I discovered that I can't even get *me* to do what I want, let alone control anyone or anything else.

This time I decided to offer my predicament as a topic at the meeting I attended that night. My fellow AA members suggested that if I couldn't control my own will I might try turning it over to God as I understood him. They also suggested that it was not what I was doing but what I was *not* doing that had me trapped. Did I ever go out in bad weather to buy booze? Yes, I did. Why let the weather stop me from going to a meeting! Did I think my relationship with my family was going to get better by crying about it? No, I didn't. Did I think they were going to change how they related to me just because I had sobered up? No. Maybe I had better change what I expected from them and from myself. Did I think a job was going to fall into my lap by just reading the want ads? No, I was going to have to go out and apply where help was wanted.

I began to realize that I was going to have to put what I decided into practice and that I needed help doing it. When I prayed before going to sleep that night, I included my usual thanksgiving for another day without a drink and then asked God to take my uncontrollable will into his care along with my unmanageable life.

When I woke the next morning, I got dressed and went to church. I asked again for God to take my will into his care and guide me through whatever I had to do. When I arrived home, my husband had left for work and the children (now teen-agers) were up getting ready for school. One of them asked me where I had been. I replied that I had been to church. Another remarked that I'd been going to church all my life and it hadn't made any difference.

I didn't answer.

They squabbled over who got the bathroom

next, expressed anger at the dog hair on their clothes and in general bemoaned their fate as children of an alcoholic . . . me specifically.

Each time I wanted to interfere or defend myself, but instead I silently asked God to control my will and guide me.

I did not respond nor did I run to my room and cry. It was not easy, but I felt quite different after they had all left—more in control of myself. I didn't spend the rest of the day mentally forecasting the possible confrontations that might occur when they returned home. I wasn't worrying ahead of time about something that may or may not even happen.

That was a change for me, and I could feel the difference. After many months of meetings, many cups of coffee with my sponsor, and a growing belief that I truly was powerless over people, places, and things, I found it easier to turn *our* will and *our* lives—my entire family's, not just mine—over to the care of God as I understood him.

Along with gradually letting go of control, I also began to learn who or what I was or was not responsible for.

I am responsible today for my own sobriety by choosing not to drink, and God is the source of power that allows me to live out that choice.

I am responsible for carrying the message of recovery to other suffering alcoholics, but I am not responsible for whether or not they choose recovery over death or insanity.

I am responsible for having set a bad example by providing false values for my children when they were young, but I am not responsible if they choose to follow that example as adults when they have other choices and a different example from me to imitate now.

I am responsible for my failures and shortcomings, but I am not responsible for anyone else's.

I am responsible for my choices, but I am not responsible for how someone else feels about them.

I did not learn these lessons easily or quickly, nor do I always remember them every day.

I also needed to learn that other people, places and things should not be allowed to control me. Blaming others (trying to make them responsible) keeps the focus off me and what I am doing or not doing and deepens the idea that I am the victim of someone else's behavior. It was what kept me from trying to change and prevented me from seeing recovery as a possibility.

It was only when I could look at the end result (*I was in pain!*) and forget about blaming me or someone else for how I got that way, that I could begin to think of looking for help. The practice of "shame and blame" is a large stumbling block to conversion and self-acceptance because it targets persons, not problems. As long as I attempted to make other persons, places, or things responsible for my life, they had power over me. Unless they changed, I couldn't change either.

The same is true of others who blame me or try to make me responsible for their lives. In essence, we say to each other, "You are in control of me, and I will have to wait until you stop doing what you are doing or being who you are being before I can take control of my own life."

This change in me was a painful process for the whole family. I did come home from the rehab unit sober and struggling to stay that way, but my family could only remember what I was like before. They had no experience of anything different, so their expectations that everything would be the same were not unnatural.

I think they wanted it to be different but needed time to come to believe, just as I was trying to do. Then came the realization that none of us could relate any longer to each other as we had done in the past. The changes I was trying to make in my life were going to affect them as well as me.

When I attended a meeting right in my own neighborhood for the first time, there was some anxiety that I would be seen and everyone would know that their wife and mother was an alcoholic. It was difficult enough to live with my own shame at that time. When I tried to carry theirs too, it was devastating.

I went to the meeting anyway, but I wasn't sure whether or not I was doing them an injustice. Fortunately, when I shared my feelings at the meeting, I was given some practical suggestions for putting first things first—and the first thing to be considered was my sobriety. I had to unload everyone else's feelings and lives, turn all of them over to my Higher Power, and proceed to focus on myself and what I was trying to accomplish for me.

This is not an easy thing to do with those you

do love and feel responsible for, but it is necessary. It is one more step toward not trying to control others or letting them control you. It is an invitation to acceptance of each other as we are.

Now that I've mentioned the word "acceptance," let me say that I had a very difficult time with it because I thought it meant the same as approval. Acceptance is *not* approval. Acceptance simply means taking people, places and things as they are—not as I would like them to be. It does not mean that I agree with or approve of them as they are, but it frees me from the responsibility for trying to change them. That lifts an enormous burden off my back and gives me the needed time to work the Twelve Steps—which are really about changing my life and being powerless over yours. It allows us to be free and accountable for ourselves.

As I tried to practice these principles which my sponsor and fellow AA members had shared with me, my relationship with my family got better—at least from my side. I no longer felt anxiety and stress even though we all seemed to be going in different directions. I no longer felt anxious about whether they approved or disapproved of my "new life." Life was definitely better than when I had tried to do everything my way.

I discovered that when I gave my will and my life over to God's care, he would take control. When I balked at following his plan, God would relinquish control. If I tried to make God responsible for my failures and shortcomings, he would somehow find a way to let me know what I was *not* doing. The more I was able to turn my will and life over and leave it in God's care, the more I seemed to be in control of it.

All my previous experiences had taught me that other people wanted control of me for their own benefit. Now I seemed to have found someone who was willing to take control of my will and my life for *my* benefit. Very unusual being, this God I was coming to understand!

I was now making four AA meetings a week—not three—in all kinds of weather. Somehow, that fourth meeting just slipped in there without my even thinking about it. Since things had gotten better in several areas of my life, I decided I had better remind my Higher Power that I still needed a job, so I turned that over too.

I got all the want ads I had cut out of the paper and began making phone calls. The first three responses were that the jobs had already been filled. Feeling somewhat discouraged, I thought maybe it would be better to wait for the following Sunday's paper before making any more calls, but something inside of me kept urging me to contact all the companies from the want ads I had clipped.

Eleven phone calls later, I had made four appointments for interviews in the next three days. Two weeks then passed, and I hadn't heard from any of the prospective employers. I started my usual mental process of wondering what was wrong with them, what was wrong with me, how would we be able to keep paying tuition and the other bills if I didn't get a job soon.

After I had stirred up enough anxiety and frustration to last the rest of the day, I went to a meeting that evening. I asked if we could talk about the Third Step and what to do if you turned your will over and things still didn't seem to be going right. Yes, I seemed to be handling the relationship with the family a little bit better, but what I really needed was a job. I remember one person sharing a similar experience and stating that she was still the one who was defining what "going right" meant. She said she now knew that if she had really turned her will and her life over to God, she was going to have to let God decide what "going right" meant.

I talked to her after the meeting and I said it sounded like I was supposed to just passively sit and wait for something to happen. She said, "No, that's not what I meant. How about getting another paper, cutting out some more ads and making some more phone calls?" The following Sunday, I ransacked the want ads. Monday produced seven more phone calls and four more appointments. The following week, one of the companies called me back and asked if I could start work on the next Monday.

I was delighted and thankful—at first. Then I started thinking about the other seven jobs I didn't get. This one paid the least salary, had the fewest benefits, and was in a location that would require me to take three buses to get to work. I really tried to feel good about getting a job, but I am sure God knew I was a little disappointed about his choice.

But I remembered that when I had been offered the help of the rehab unit I had wanted to nit-pick to determine how the help should be given, so I decided to leave my will and life in God's care and go with the job I had been offered. After all, I had asked for a job and I got a job. My first day at work, I decided to discuss the salary issue with the boss. I agreed to start for the salary being offered and proposed that if I could prove that I could do all he wanted done and then some he would give me a review and reconsideration of the salary I had originally requested. He said he would in six months; I asked him to make it six weeks. We both agreed on three months. After one month, he came to my desk, expressed his satisfaction with my work and gave me the raise.

Shortly after that, my husband lost his job of 30 years. He began to drive me to work in the morning, pick me up at night and try to deal with his deep sense of betrayal and rejection—and job hunt—in between. I wondered occasionally if God had a weird sense of humor, because we were back to one salary again with all the same expenses. My husband was out of work for a year-and-a-half, but somehow we made it. Money came from where I least expected it. Someone I had loaned money to before I was married (and whom I never expected to hear from again) suddenly looked me up and paid me back. Then we got a notice from the bank about accounts with no activity being taken over by the state, and there had been no activity on an account with our name on it for several years. I didn't know we had a savings account left, but I started searching through all my papers and found a passbook showing several hundred dollars in it. I mailed it in and they added six years worth of interest! A job finally opened for my husband. It was located so that he could still drop me off at work every morning and pick me up every night. His new job provided good enough benefits so that my lack of them was no longer a big concern.

Of course, it's easy to look back on life and see how everything fell into place and was "going right" all along. It is much harder to trust that it will happen when you aren't there yet.

The Third Step isn't something I've been able to do once and it's over with. I have to keep making this decision to turn my life and my will over to God again and again, especially when I'm in a new area of my life, an area that I haven't dealt with before, a place that is still likely to be filled with denial and rationalization.

When I look back over my life, I can see that God has willed much better things for me than I ever did, has produced more good, lasting results than I ever produced, and has loved me far more than I could love myself. How true it is that "deep are the riches and the wisdom and the knowledge of God!" and "who has known the mind of the Lord? Or who has been his counselor?" (Rom 11:33-34). God has been willing to take my powerlessness, uncontrollable will and unmanageable life into his care when even I didn't want them. My Higher Power seems to have not only admitted but lovingly accepted the fact that this earthen vessel came from his potter's hands and so it gets easier for me to accept it too...even though I know he's not finished with me yet.

I think the story of the miracle at the wedding feast in Cana is a successful Third Step story (Jn 2:1-10). Sure, turning water into wine is a miracle, but after reading this story in the light of my Third Step attempts, I think there was something even more miraculous going on.

Mary simply says to Jesus, "They have no wine,"

and she apparently expects that he can and will do something about it. No instructions about how to take care of it. She tells the servants, "Do whatever he tells you," and obviously expects them to do it. Jesus tells them to fill the stone jars with water, and they do it without asking why. He then tells them to draw some out and take it to the headwaiter. If this is just water, they could lose their jobs, but they do it, obviously expecting that the water is somehow different, without knowing what has been done. Everyone in this story is carrying out a decision to turn his or her will and life over to the care of another!

Reflection Questions

1. What do you do that you don't want to do?

2. Whom or what in your life do you truly trust?

3. If you surrendered control, how do you think you would feel?

For now we see in a mirror dimly

(1COR 13:12)

Step Four

Made a searching and fearless moral inventory of ourselves.

$\mathcal{M}$y sponsor had persuaded me to tell my story at a few meetings, and what became apparent to me was that I had an abundance of "how I was," a little bit of "what happened," and not a whole lot of "how I am today."

Certainly, things were better than they used to be, but I still felt like I was mostly groping and searching and questioning. Shouldn't I be farther along than this? Shouldn't I have changed more? Shouldn't I feel better about myself? There was something missing, though I did not know what it was.

With this in mind, my sponsor felt I might be ready for the Fourth Step. I would be introduced to my "roots"—those things that seek life in the underground darkness, my connections to earthly things. I also needed to find what enabled me to be pulled upward out of the earth, what nourished me from above and gave me life and identity beyond my roots.

A "moral inventory" would help me sort out what was good and what was evil—just as a business inventory counts and sorts out what is salable and beneficial from what is damaged or defective and should be discarded.

What I discovered was that I was harboring a great deal of anger and resentment, jealousy, hate, self-pity and much more.

I had been coming from a perspective where I had seen me as good and others as bad, me as victim and others as persecutors, me as right and others as wrong. It is not uncommon to discover that I would now reverse that perspective and experience a great deal of shame.

But shame attacks persons, not defects, and that is *not* the purpose of Step Four. What I really needed to experience was a healthy dose of *guilt*, which—though very uncomfortable—is meant to lead me to attack my defects and shortcomings.

If I was supposed to self-destruct, I could have kept drinking. The purpose of this step (and the whole AA program) is to help reconstruct lives and "selves" within the framework of sobriety and change.

My sponsor suggested that I follow the format outlined in the AA Big Book. We "search for those things that have caused our failure. Being convinced that self, manifested in various ways, was what had defeated us, we considered its common manifestations."

I was to list the people, places, things that have made me angry. I started with a "grudge list" and then identified what part of me had been wounded. Was it my self-esteem, my pride? What was it that weakened my self-confidence and brought fear, the fear then breeding anger and the anger often turning into resentment? The more resentment got a foothold, the more prone I was to hate and self-pity. This was as far as I had gotten while drinking. It is generally the situation for most of us.

Now I was to take it a step further. Never mind what was done to me—real or imagined. I needed to pay attention to my *response*, because that is what would be "manifested."

I began to write on my inventory sheet my character defects. I had seen the effect they have had on my life. My sponsor wisely stopped me and instructed me to go no further with the list of "defects" until I had uncovered some of my "assets"—something I initially had difficulty with.

We reviewed some of the areas of my life that seemed to have gotten better to determine what was different. I had certainly come to believe that God loved me no matter what I had done, and that helped me to focus on those who loved me rather than those who didn't. I had become more accepting of others' behavior, without having to respond to it at all. I no longer had to immediately accept or reject everything anyone, including myself, thought or said about me as truth; I just needed to let those opinions be a possibility. I could add faith, acceptance, patience and understanding to my asset side of the list.

I began to get a clearer idea of what I was trying to achieve: Whenever a problem arose and I began to feel pressured or threatened, I had to strongly resist the responses that had become habits and begin to realize what I could do instead. It was important to treat the wound effectively, rather than spend time determining how or by whom it had been inflicted. While I wouldn't refuse treatment for a broken leg and permanently cripple myself just so I could blame "the kid who knocked me off my bike," I had always insisted upon crippling myself emotionally by hanging onto my past hurts so I could feel victimized and free of responsibility for my life. I needed to learn how to "shake the dust from [my] feet" (Lk 9:5) and let go of the past so that it can't keep controlling me.

For me, Step Four would not have been possible without the love and acceptance that had been given by my fellow AA members, my sponsor, and the God I had come to understand on the first three steps. There almost seemed to be a parallel between my willingness to change and broaden my understanding of God and others and my willingness to change and broaden my understanding of myself.

Each time I stopped blaming God or others for what was happening to me, I was more likely to discover how I was causing much of my own distress. Though God was more deeply within me and beside me at all times, I was also beginning to recognize that he was separate and distinct from me. Though God had knowledge of good and evil, he was able to always choose good. I could be deceived and confused about which was which, so my choices were not guaranteed. God had power apart from me that I did not have apart from him.

My experience has been that the Fourth Step allows me to form a new understanding of my humanity just as the Second, Third, and Eleventh steps allow me to attain a new "understanding" of God. The hard part, in both cases, is getting rid of the old ideas and being open to new possibilities.

I had been honest and serious about the first three steps and had already discovered that I didn't have to drink as a response to reality. I had been freed from the compulsion for an "instant solution" and had allowed life to simply be as it is—under someone else's control. I had come to grips with some of my puzzling behavior, but I still didn't really understand why I behaved the way I did.

I learned very early in Step Two about the insanity of holding resentments. I would lay awake nights rehashing the hurts that I felt others had inflicted on me. I would mentally hate them and judge them and want to hurt them back. They had a very strong hold on my response to life, which kept me awake at night while they were sleeping soundly. Who was paying the price?

I can remember how I felt when I had failed at something I was trying to do, including my attempts to stop drinking on my own. My learned response was to blame others. I had to go back to drinking because of others' behavior. The people of AA were very blunt in their questions about this perspective of mine. "Did they — those other people who are at fault — tie you down and pour the booze down your throat? If not, then you are responsible for your choice to drink!"

I needed to own my responses to frustration, failure, disappointment and pain. When I finally did that, I could consider other alternatives. I was told not to make a decision about what to do without having at least three choices. This solid piece of advice is geared to stop me from instantly grabbing the known and taking time to learn new ways of doing things. And it took time. Just admitting I had a defect did not make it go away. Sometimes, it seemed as if I was doing nothing, and sometimes—surprisingly—that is exactly what I should be doing.

Fear played a large part in my unwillingness to try the unknown. Fear is another major wound that needs to be healed because it stifles our spirit. There are people in this world who will reject us for who we are, what we believe, how we behave—but there are also some who won't. At first contact with AA, I didn't know which kind of people I was sharing myself with, and so I was afraid to put myself on the line. I had that kind of fear at my first meetings. I felt I would be judged and found unworthy, because that was how I felt about myself. Instead, I was greeted with a warmth and understanding I had never experienced before. I would never have known the genuine fellowship of AA if I had not risked possible rejection. The reluctance to "let go of [my] old ideas" is mostly fear of the unknown. My old ideas were all I was and had, and I convinced myself that they were the truth.

When I came to AA, I was convinced that the God I knew and worshiped at the time was the "real" one, and if others had a different "description" they were wrong. My definition of God was gradually changed by taking a chance that what others were telling me about his desire to help me might be true. It was gradually changed when I could get over my fear that God only wanted to punish me for all my sins.

When I think about it today, I compare my old approach to staying away from a doctor when I am sick because the doctor might punish me for being sick. I realize now that my major "sin" was probably belittling God, imagining him as some kind of cruel ogre, and not being able to really love and respect him.

This was also a defense mechanism to keep God out of my life in a real way, because if I ever did come to understand God as he truly is, I would have to change, and that was another thing I was often afraid of. I no longer would be able to use my fear of God as an excuse for my spiritual behavior.

Fear is a powerful emotion and can create all kinds of obstacles to love and growth. I am no longer afraid of God. I no longer doubt that God will go to any lengths to save me. I no longer doubt that I am precious to God and believe that there is not a moment of my life—past, present or future—when he is not present. This is a different response to God that is much more beneficial to me than anything I ever knew before.

Through the Fourth Step, I learned that many of my opinions of myself and other people had been formed the same way as my image of God: through gossip, jealousy, pride, self-serving motives, other peoples' experiences. When my maternal grandfather would hear anyone putting someone else down because of who they were or what they believed, he would say, "If you have to blow out someone else's candle to make your own look bright, there is something wrong with your candle." Blowing out other people's candles is not uncommon in people who are trying to gain some self-esteem, some recognition, and perhaps even some occupational or financial gain. We do the "see-saw" routine: If I put you down, then I will be up. If I can find others worse than me, then I can feel good about me.

Communicating other people's shortcomings through gossip while being blind to our own faults is an ineffective way of building up one's own ego. It changes nothing about us and always has to be repeated each time another is perceived as threatening us. It is the proof that we humans do indeed "see the speck in your neighbor's eye and miss the log in your own" (Lk 6:41).

Comparing and competing seem to be two of our national pastimes in the self-image struggle. Yet even this ineffective characteristic of mine was put to good use in my inventory. This is part of the purpose of Step Four—to turn our shortcomings around and see a positive use for them. AA taught me that I only have to compare myself to myself—how I was then and what I am like today. Self-image does not improve by putting others down, by denying my shortcomings and defects, by constantly seeking affirmation from others, or by holding positions of status and power and wealth. My self-image improved when I could allow my wounds to be healed, change my behavior, make progress in becoming human, and accept and even become grateful for the fact that there is someone greater than me, someone who loves me unconditionally and has the power to help me grow.

Only when I could truly accept who I am right now, knowing there is still more to come, could I begin to love myself and others.

In AA I was told not to take other people's inventory, but my sponsor told me to go ahead and take everyone's inventory. But then I was to go home and stand in front of my mirror and accuse myself of everything I thought about those other people. Projecting my faults onto others was so natural to my humanity, but it kept me thinking the defects were "out there," when in fact they were in me. It didn't mean that those other people didn't have the same shortcomings, but the purpose of this step was to help me discover that I have them.

In AA the goal is to strive for spiritual progress, not spiritual perfection. If I ever thought I had reached perfection, I'd be finished—in more ways than one. Progress is preventive maintenance. It's taking your car to the mechanic when your wheel first starts wobbling, rather than waiting for the wheel to fall off. It's putting that guy-wire on the tree when it first starts to grow crooked, rather than waiting until it is too big to redirect. It's calling your sponsor when you first start feeling pulled back to your old thinking and drinking ways, rather than after you've taken a drink. It's surrounding yourself with an environment that will invite you to faith and hope, change and growth, responsibility and honesty with yourself.

Certainly we have to operate in the "real" world, but we can cope if we have a firm spiritual foundation to build upon and strong principles to guide us. We can learn to "set our minds on things that are above, not on things that are on earth" (Col 3:2) a little bit at a time, one day at a time.

Reflection Questions

1. What keeps you from being truly honest with yourself? With others?

2. If you let go of past hurts and injuries, what might happen?

3. What would you need to build a "safe environment" for yourself?

Who do you say that I am?

(Mt 16:15)

Step Five

Admitted to God, to ourselves,
and to another human being,
the exact nature of our wrongs.

had done my inventory. Now I had to admit my faults to someone else. It was like my initial attempts at admitting to myself that I was an alcoholic. It was all in my head and on my lips, but the real acceptance of my defects had not sunk into my being yet.

Although I may be able to convince myself that I have no defects, even I knew that I would not be able to convince anyone else. Besides, I needed the observations and reflections of others to uncover both my assets and my defects, with the understanding that these people can offer "possibilities" that I cannot see. I have to neither accept nor reject their reflections; I just add them to my list of "possibilities."

Yet I balked at Step Five even more than at Step Four.

I began one night with my prayer of thanksgiving for another sober day and offered some of my inventory for divine consideration:

I am full of pride, God.

I don't want to be an alcoholic.

I don't deserve to be an alcoholic.

I never intended to become an alcoholic;

I was just looking for help. Everyone thinks it's my fault and that I chose to be this way.

You know that inside of me I'm still fighting against admitting that I can't manage my own life and that I need help.

I feel humiliation and shame.

Why didn't you stop this from happening to me?

Why didn't you show me the right way to live before I got this far?

I just knelt there by my bed. I would have understood if the ceiling had opened up and a voice had said, "You viper!" (Mt 3:7). "You white-washed tomb! You hypocrite!" (Mt 23:27-28), but I didn't hear anything. There was a strange feeling of confusion that God had not responded as I expected him to, but there was also a strange feeling of peace. The only thing I wanted to do was cry, so I did.

I continued this process for many weeks, including more and more of my defects—sometimes rationalizing and defending myself against them and sometimes just verbalizing them. What I considered to be an asset of mine even crept in once in a while, maybe in an attempt to persuade God that there was something in me worth saving.

I allowed myself to look at me—at least the parts that had become visible—and share that with "God as I understood him." But I came to realize that I still didn't really understand God. Why hadn't he judged the rightness and wrongness of my inventory? Why hadn't he compared his wholeness and goodness to my brokenness and badness?

I had the same kind of eerie feeling that I had experienced at my first AA meetings; if shame and blame wasn't the thrust, what was God after?

I came to understand much, much later that I was not met with shame and blame and rejection simply because I had not inflicted it on myself. I came expecting God to think and feel and respond according to human judgments, and in these brief encounters he had instead allowed me to think and feel and respond as he does—with acceptance of the truth.

By admitting them to God I was simultaneously admitting these things to myself, though I still didn't know what to do about a lot of it. I still didn't have better responses to many of the people, places and things that are part of my life, but I felt more secure about backing off the dysfunctional reactions and trying to learn new ones. I definitely became more interested in the healing of my wounds than in denying them and suffering needlessly.

Yes, the pain of the remedy may hurt more than the wound at first, but as the relief becomes more permanent in the end you suffer less. Admitting the exact nature of my wrongs meant pulling off all the protective devices I had wrapped my "self" in. It meant getting rid of words like "but" or "because" when I was using them to blame others for my defects. It meant getting rid of my judgments about how life, circumstances and other people should be and learning to deal with them as they really are.

And most of all, that included my judgments about myself. I needed to accept me as I was and still leave lots of room for who I could become.

I shared all this with God, and God loved me still. When it came time to share myself with another human being as Step Five suggests, however, I was much more nervous. Whom could I trust? Was there anyone who would understand?

I went back to my sponsor for help. I expressed my fears about being able to remain really honest if I felt I was being judged or rejected. She suggested that I try to find someone who would be more interested in helping me recover from the past than condemning me to live in it. She reminded me that Step Five asks me to deal with the nature of my wrongs, not a blow-by-blow description of everything I ever did. "Just share your story," she said, "about what you have learned about yourself and what you would like to do with that information."

I instinctively knew that this was going to be a very important part of my recovery and growth. Naturally, I wanted to find someone who would understand what I was trying to do and support me in doing it. I needed to feel confident that whoever I went to would focus on accepting and helping me as a person. I thought I knew someone.

"Barb? Are you going to be home this afternoon? I could sure use a haircut!"

"Great! I haven't seen you since you came home from wherever you were. About one o'clock, OK?"

My "confession" turned out to be not only a necessary step, but a truly *good* experience. *(The "lost sheep" bleated away and Barb just kept shearing!)* I told her I had been in an alcoholism treatment center. She said she was happy for me that I had gotten help. I told her it was still hard for me to talk about some things. She told me she was honored that I had chosen to share it with her. I told her I was supposed to try to talk about "the exact nature of my wrongs" and asked if she was willing to listen to that.

She said she thought she would be helped by whatever I had to say.

With both Barb and a priest that I went to later, I was not disappointed. Both times, I prayed for God to lead me to the right person. Both times, I was blessed. I did not need someone who was going to feel sorry for me over the pain of my past indiscretions or the pain of my present struggles. I needed someone who could rejoice in the healing that was in progress. I needed someone who knew me but who had not been directly affected by my drinking so he or she could understand that I *had* a problem, not that I *was* a problem. I needed someone who had or was seeking a sense of purpose for their own life, who could understand self-examination and the necessary changes required to live out that purpose.

If I had run off to the people whose names popped into my mind first, I think I would have been looking for pity, pardon or punishment, the things I offered myself when I was drinking. Those names that came immediately to my mind were perhaps just another attempt by me to stay with what I already knew rather than pushing beyond. I later had my suspicions confirmed. When some of these people did find out about my membership in AA, I found them to be somewhat less than supportive about my need for the AA fellowship and my reliance on it. The concern seemed to be that I was "betraying" God by putting my faith in a "man-made" program and they had doubts about the outcome. Theirs was the judgment and the sense of pity that is frequently offered to "outcasts" by those who know about the power of God but have never needed it for themselves.

"Here, let me brush the hair off your shirt," Barb joked. "Get it? No hair shirt for you! What you did yesterday doesn't matter. What you are doing now is wonderful and I hope I can learn some of it from you."

"Thanks, Barb," I responded. "Thanks for the haircut—and for not shaving my head! Can we talk again? I need someone who understands."

PS: "Drunkalogs" are sometimes heard at AA meetings—long, drawn out stories of what we did when we were drinking. It is much easier to deal with these, and some of them are downright funny, when we're not engaged in drinking anymore. But to deal with the "exact nature of our wrongs" is not the same. It means finding out the root problem, the reason why we did what we did. Saying "I'm only repeating what someone else told me" is easier than admitting that I gossip. Putting someone else down and excusing it by highlighting one of their defects as justification is much easier than admitting our own jealousy or lack of self-esteem. All of us have to try to own the jealousy, the gossip, the low self-esteem and the behavior it brings out of us as well as the effect it may have on others. Sharing our secret-self with God and another person is not easy. Some reject the idea of Step Five as unnecessary. I was comfortable for a while thinking I had successfully dealt with my fears, my dishonesty, my pride, but they were the very things that cropped up when I contemplated the Fifth Step. They weren't gone and they had not been forgotten!

PPS: I found that "a disappointing experience" is the way to describe choosing someone to confide in who is not able to detach from his or her own judgment and ego. It goes like this: Someone who seems understanding and helpful for a while is unable to keep confidences or winds up using these confidences for his or her own advantage. I would urge you—even knowing the pain that is suffered in such an instance—not to let it stop you from taking the risk again. Don't let someone else's defects and shortcomings become an excuse for not confronting your own and accomplishing the good you owe yourself. Self-sufficiency and isolation are two responses that will keep you from spiritual progress.

Reflection Questions

1. It is very difficult for you to admit that you . . . .

2. Who are the people in your life you could confide in?

3. If you shared your defects with one or more of these people, how might they respond? Are you willing to find out what really happens?

Deliver me from the hand of my enemies

(PS 31:16)

Step Six

> *Were entirely ready to have God remove all these defects of character.*

Step Seven

> *Humbly asked him to remove our shortcomings.*

$\mathcal{G}$etting acquainted with my human condition was the spiritual equivalent of being diagnosed with a crippling disease. But I learned through the wisdom of a friend that how I handled the disease would depend on whether *I have it* or *it has me*. To be able to accept the fact that I have defects without being limited to them became part of my understanding of salvation. Knowing that other responses are available, even if I didn't (and still don't always) know how to use them yet, was enough to allow me to move in another direction.

Even then, I knew from my previous experience of admitting powerlessness, insanity and the need to let someone else guide my will that change was not going to be easy—but it was going to be possible.

Having identified and shared my inventory with God, myself, and another human being as honestly and completely as I could, I needed to make a decision about what I wanted to do with the use of my defects—what I have come to define as my "shortcomings."

I found that I was ready to become vulnerable to life instead of protecting myself from it. Two valuable pieces of knowledge grew out of this decision:

1. The fact that I am an alcoholic was not going to be removed, but the condition of having to drink had been.

2. The fact that I am human and imperfect was not going to be removed, but the denial of that truth had been.

I needed to become acutely aware of my learned responses before I came to manifest them externally. For example, when I was feeling "instant anger," I learned to pray to have it removed as an outward expression and to ask God instead for a better solution.

Initially, it took a lot of time before I could examine what I was angry about, what part of me felt threatened or wounded, or how I could better handle these situations. With daily practice, though, I found I could locate the source more quickly and respond in a way that was more beneficial to my own healing and growth. Even so there are still times I don't seem to be able to come up with a better thing to do—except to not do what I feel like doing and to do "nothing" in its place.

Feelings of wanting to retaliate or get even—the children of resentment—were two other areas where I had to back off and pray. My prayer would be something like this: "Lord Jesus, I may be able to hurt those who have hurt me, but I will have to negate my efforts to incorporate Steps Six and Seven into my life and I will just add more pain to already wounded relationships. You did indeed take away the sins of the world by absorbing them into yourself and not releasing them back onto others. You knew Peter would deny you and Judas would betray you, but you didn't stop them from doing it. You just acknowledged your awareness and acceptance of their behavior. I have incidents like that in my life, too. Lord, maybe I serve your will in those cases by not reacting to those who have hurt me in some way. Help me to do your will."

Today I would rather run the risk that those I have chosen as friends may hurt me than isolate and protect myself from them.

When jealousy and envy pop up, I know I need to take time to determine what position or possession I am guarding so diligently or what of someone else's possessions do I want so badly that I can't get it out of my mind. So often in the past I would become miserable thinking about what I had and didn't want or what I wanted and didn't have, but through Steps Six and Seven I learned that jealousy and envy don't motivate me to change anything about myself. Since I cannot control people, places and things, there is no guarantee that what I have will not be taken from me, and there will always be someone who has more status, power and possessions than I have. I need to have jealousy and envy removed because they can keep me hanging onto or thinking I need the wrong things. And, even more harmful, they can keep me from being truly grateful for what I have today.

Like alcohol, my defects will always be a choice that I have available, but I now have other options also. Now I know there are quite a few better ways of responding. Like physical exercise, the options that I use most frequently (my "tallcomings") will be strengthened and the neglected ones (my "shortcomings") will be weakened. While I cannot remove my own defects of character and shortcomings, I learned that I can turn them over to the care of "God as I understand him," and I believe God will teach me how to replace them with something of value.

Steps Four, Five, Six and Seven have brought me to a new understanding of myself. I do not have a choice about whether I want to be human and imperfect, but I do have a choice about how I feel about it and how I act on that information:

Do I want to reject my limitations and pretend I don't have them, or do I want to learn how to do all I can do within them?

Do I want to think that everything ends where I leave off, or do I want to believe there is a power beyond me that can exceed my limitations?

I was able to grow most by concentrating on what I am *for* rather than what I am *against*:

I am *for* my sobriety, not *against* anyone else's drinking.

I am *for* gratitude for whatever I have "today," not *against* the voids that haven't been filled yet.

Though the roots of the tree are deeply anchored in the earth, the part that gives it its identity grows upward above the ground. Though my defects are what anchor my humanity to earthly things, I too would prefer to grow upward and find my identity in what is above.

Reflection Questions

1. If you give up your defects and shortcomings, what will be left of you?

2. Does being "human" disappoint or relieve you?

3. What are you for?

Forgive us our debts

(MT 6:9-12)

Step Eight

Made a list of all persons we had harmed, and became willing to make amends to them all.

Step Nine

Made direct amends to such people whenever possible, except when to do so would injure them or others.

*T*he first seven steps had been primarily focused on me—identifying my problem, accepting help for myself, determining those characteristics that keep me from making progress in my recovery and—finally—wanting to free myself of them. In the past, I was willing to do whatever had to be done to maintain the world I had created, and I would let nothing stand in my way. My concentration was not on whom I might have hurt but on who might hurt or hinder me.

Again, there was a similarity between then and now in that "myself" was as far as I ever got when I was drinking. Now I was being asked in Steps Eight and Nine to go beyond that and face the fact that others were involved in my pain and were affected by my lifestyle. I had needed to spend recovery time with myself and my Higher Power, but now I needed to look outward and see myself in relationship to others. If I couldn't, I would continue to live in a self-contained and self-created world, and even though this new one was better than the old one, it was still not reality. Now I needed to be willing to stay out of God's way so he could help me see others as he had helped me see myself. It would not be easy.

By now, I had become familiar with the idea that the AA program doesn't work if it's just kept in the head. I had set a new direction for my life and it included being responsible for the chaos and possible harm I caused in others' lives as well as my own. The Eighth and Ninth Steps were meant to help me determine whether I really am willing "to go to any lengths" to insure my recovery.

Even beyond that, the goal was to become a person who can give service to God and others. These steps are firmly based in the Scriptures: "So when you are offering your gift at the altar, if you remember that your brother or sister has something against you, leave your gift there before the altar and go; first be reconciled to your brother or sister, and then come and offer your gift" (Mt 5:23-24). *(It would seem that offering homage to God is not an acceptable substitute for healing the wounds that exist between humans!)*

The list of persons I had harmed was pretty much compiled during previous steps. Becoming willing and able to make amends to them was another hurdle that I knew would be painful to leap. "Start with yourself," I was told, "and remember we are talking about harmed, not hurt. There may be many who felt pain, but we're looking for those whose lives have been damaged in some way because of your choices."

I had certainly damaged my relationships as a wife, mother, and friend. I had created an environment of insecurity and mistrust for those around me and cut myself off from them. Their feelings about me would not change overnight just because I stopped drinking, just as my feelings about me did not change just because I stopped drinking. It had taken a long time, many meetings, and the seven previous steps to convince me that I was not the same person I used to be. It would take a long time for others to believe I was different, and some might never believe it because they might not be able to get past their own wounds.

I would have to continue to be different, whether they believed it or not. I could not let the reminders of yesterday determine what I would do today, because I no longer wanted to harm myself or others any more than I already had.

My children were my biggest challenge in Steps Eight and Nine. I had harmed my children most because they had learned to imitate my values and behavior. For example: When life gets tough, escape from it. When you are hurting, blame someone else. Point the finger at others so they look bad and you look good. Let your feelings control you instead of you controlling them. Look at which choice would be worse, not what choice could be better.

Yes, they had seen some good example from me, too, but the more easily learned ones seemed to accompany my convenient, self-serving attitudes.

They were younger then and more inclined to just follow in my footsteps. Now they are adults facing the same challenges I have had to face—change the parts of their lives that aren't helpful to them, learn new values if their old ones are built on ego and short-term gratification, seek a Power greater than themselves to show them the meaning of love.

It isn't any easier for them to give up their learned responses or come to a new understanding of God and themselves than it is for me. I cannot undo the pain my children may have already suffered; I can only try to relate to them with the values and attitudes I have learned and continue to learn every day.

I approached Step Nine with a conviction that if I did what I was supposed to—acknowledge who I had been and who I am trying to be today—everything would be all right. The first time I went to my family and acknowledged the behavior that I felt had been harmful to them, I was pretty much met with silence. I had done what I was supposed to do, but I didn't feel that everything was all right. Over the next months, I heard remarks comparing my "absences" to attend AA meetings with my mental and emotional "absences" when I was drinking. There were comments that I was still only thinking of myself and not showing concern for their needs and feelings. There were occasional statements that things were better when I was drinking.

On the other hand, there were periodic offers to drive me to a meeting so I didn't have to wait for a bus in bad weather. There were intermittent observations that I seemed to be happier and that we, as a family, didn't have the atmosphere of insecurity we had lived with in the past.

My family's responses—and my own—pretty much ran the gamut of available human emotions and objective logic. All kinds of possibilities for different ways of relating to each other opened up— some very tense, some very tender.

I learned, again, from their experience to stop trying to define what "all right" meant, since what was right for me was not always right for someone else. I learned that each of us would have to determine who we could be for the others. I learned that we all have to deal with our pain in the way we know how—at least until we can learn better and more healing ways.

It is not easy to go to others and own up to the

behavior that may have caused them harm. It is the fear of the unknown again, because we don't know how people will respond. They might forgive and even offer encouragement, or they might accept our admission of wrongs as confirmation that they had a right to be hostile and even spiteful. In either case, it is not our job to take responsibility for how they react. We hope for forgiveness and the opportunity to set things right, of course, but their response is not the focus of Steps Eight and Nine. It is our ability to sincerely acknowledge what we have done in the past and our willingness to make amends, to change our behavior, to heal the relationships that count. It is not enough to regret what we have done only in our heads and hearts, for that will lead us to admission but not true acceptance. We must actually go to these people and ask forgiveness and then show by our actions that we mean it.

One note of caution. There may have been incidents in our past lives that would harm others now if we told about them. If our families or friends are unaware of these episodes, this would not be the time to bring them up. There has probably already been enough damage to our relationships by the known alcoholic behavior. That doesn't mean we write these incidents off as insignificant, but they would be handled better by discussing them with our sponsors or ordained ministers. The Big Book is quite clear about not ducking the responsibility to face painful and difficult wrongs. The aim of Steps Eight and Nine, however, is to protect others from further harm, not to tell them everything we have ever done.

These steps have allowed me to make progress

toward that sanity which lets me see the reality of the past as well as the present. They helped me clarify again that who I was yesterday, who I am today, and who I can become tomorrow are all the same person.

Reflection Questions

1. In what way have you damaged relationships that were important to you?

2. How can you make amends without causing further harm?

3. What does it mean that who you were yesterday, who you are today, and who you can become tomorrow are all the same person?

Let us run with perseverance the race that is set before us

(Heb 2:1)

Step Ten

*Continued to take personal inventory
and when we were wrong
promptly admitted it.*

*M*y defects have been, are, and will always be with me as potential choice. Though I don't really want to, I do still choose them sometimes and I must be willing to admit that. The Tenth Step says I must *promptly* admit it. Why promptly? Because I know in my heart when I have behaved wrongly, and if I don't admit it right away, my head will justify my action. I will begin to look at what the other person did to me or how the world is treating me, and I will begin to rationalize my behavior based on someone else's behavior. This is how I used to react when I was drinking and I don't want to do so now.

Instead of letting my head take me through the "serpent made me do it, the woman made me do it" routine (GN 3:12-13), I want to be able to just say, "Yes, I ate the apple".

Do I have this choice? Yes, I do. I can choose to love and forgive other persons and try to understand their shortcomings and humanity. When I do goof and let my old habits take control, I have learned that I need to be able to acknowledge it, make amends to the other, and forgive myself so I can be free again.

Since Step Ten is about my personal inventory, I know I need to concentrate on my own actions and my responses. Even if another harms me and denies it, it is better for me to own the hurt and forgive it than try to convince the other that he or she is guilty or to deny my hurt and then harbor a subconscious resentment.

In the Scripture story about the mob that wanted to stone the woman taken in adultery (Jn 8:3-11),

Jesus did not deny her sin—and apparently she didn't either. When asked who was left to condemn her she said, "no one": not the mob, not Jesus, and not herself. Notice that the woman never tried to turn the focus on the mob's behavior and their shortcomings. When Jesus made the statement, "Let the one who is without sin cast the first stone," he did turn the mob's focus onto themselves, individually. He redirected them to take their own personal inventory; he did not take it for them, nor did he let them continue to take the woman's.

When I do wrong, I want to defend myself by reminding others that they have done wrong things too. If I can convince myself that their sins are more serious than mine, I don't feel so bad about mine. I lived with that thinking for a long time. I never really felt good about myself, but at least I didn't feel as bad as I might have if I hadn't indulged in comparative justification.

Jesus seemed to be trying to get everyone to look at themselves and decide if they want to continue just choosing the lesser of two evils or to begin to seek good. The woman seemed to be able to understand the invitation to receive love and forgiveness and change her life. Was the mob able to do that? We don't know. Perhaps some of them might have, and others might have gone away angry that they had been thwarted in their attempts to shame and blame.

I have learned that it's not easy to own who I am honestly. And along with that I have learned it's not easy to admit I am wrong—promptly or otherwise. It's not easy to stop comparing and justifying yourself, but like the mob we will not get rid of our own sins by constantly attacking sin in someone else. I am able to work effectively with my defects only when I am willing to give them to God and let him teach me that they are nothing more than my assets gone astray like lost sheep.

The adultress' willingness to share her body with others was an attempt to fill her own need to be loved and wanted. But it never happened. She was just used and rejected—which was essentially the same thing she was doing to her partners. Then she met someone who showed her the futility of her behavior but loved and accepted her as a person. By accepting Jesus' forgiveness, she opened herself to the possibility of becoming something different. A person whose life had been filled with brokenness and shame and infidelity became a person of gratitude, commitment and service to others. That is the aim of the Twelve Steps.

When Jesus experienced his people "like sheep without a shepherd" (Mk 6:34), the Scripture says he began to teach them. Not judge them, nor condemn them, nor distance himself from them, but sit down right in the middle of them and teach them. That is what I believe he has done for me.

Reflection Questions

1. What happens to you when you do not promptly admit you were wrong?

2. Do you ever try to make yourself look better by attacking the faults of others? Describe one incident when you wanted to "stone" someone.

3. Can you forgive yourself? If not, what stands in the way?

Your will be done on earth

(Mt 6:9-12)

Step Eleven

*Sought through prayer and meditation
to improve our conscious contact
with God <u>as we understood him</u>,
praying only for knowledge of
his will for us and the power
to carry that out.*

$\mathcal{P}$raying only for knowledge of God's will for me certainly shortened my prayer time, because it cut out the ten thousand things I will for me (and others) —which is all I used to pray about.

During Step Eleven for me, prayer and meditation had to be completely relearned and it was quite uncomfortable at first. Instead of my usual long litany of wants and complaints that went on throughout a whole day, I found that saying, "Your will be done," took less than a second. I felt that I was praying less than before, and it took away some of my self-centered comfort level.

I did soon find myself thinking about God more often, however, waiting for the revelation of his will for me. Questions would simply appear in my mind that asked God, "What are you working on now?" or "What should I be working on now?" or "What are you doing to help this person or that person who needs help?" I found myself paying more attention to the people, places and things around me, waiting and trying to see what was unfolding in my life and others' lives.

Though I had "made a decision to turn our will and our lives" (*that's mine and everybody else's!*) over to the care of God as I understood him, I became more and more aware that I had only given him bits and pieces. A little bit of my will, a little piece of my life, usually the parts I had been able to own up to. I also turned over whatever was a problem for me. I turned over the people who annoyed me, but I still resented the fact that they had a will I couldn't control. I turned over my job, my family, the world in general; everything, in fact, except my "self."

I know it wasn't a conscious thought, but evidently I was assuming that my problems were no longer my concern. Wrong! Placing our will and our lives in the care of God is not like taking your car to the mechanic and picking it up later all repaired. His will seemed to be that I should learn how to be a mechanic! Today, I believe that it is his will for me to be willing to learn something new, something more than I know now, every day.

My aim now is to be an active participant in my life by struggling and surrendering, rejecting and accepting, doubting and believing, falling and being picked up, knocking and opening, seeking and finding, asking and receiving. Despair was my lot when I only had "either/or," when there was struggle with no surrender, when I thought I had to find all the answers myself.

Fear and insecurity came with doubting my own abilities and not believing anyone had more power than I had. Only having both the human and divine working together has brought me to an understanding of serenity.

Wholeness and balance are the result of reconciling the natural tension between heaven and earth, between the growth of the tree roots downward into the ground and the trunk and branches upward into the sky, between human limitations, imperfections and mortality and divine power, perfect goodness and eternal being. For me, that is the "cross," the intersection of my humanity and God's divinity and the struggle to keep them connected.

I do not get rid of my humanity to find God's divinity, and if I get rid of God's divinity, I have nothing to pull me toward my true humanity. The roots and the branches are one tree, just as you and I are one with God.

That is my vision today of the Genesis story. In the beginning, God created a human out of the mud and clay of the earth and covered it on the outside with his own image and likeness. At the Fall, the mud and clay covered the outside and the image and likeness of God was somehow hidden within. Our earthly religions symbolize for us the attempts to "wash off" the mud and clay in Baptism, the attempts to undo the loss of God's image in Reconciliation, the Confirmation of the presence of the now-hidden Spirit of God within our humanity.

Why didn't these sacraments work at first for me?

Maybe because I was taught what God had done for me but never learned what I was supposed to do for God—which is nothing more than being willing to let him out of his burial place in the mud and clay of my own person.

Today I accept as insanity the thinking that my humanity, my defects and shortcomings, my imperfections are what are buried and invisible to others. They were only hidden from me because I refused to acknowledge them, though everyone else could have itemized them for me!

It is now my belief that we people wear our humanity quite noticeably on the outside. It is our potential to be honest, to be whole, to be the divine image and likeness that we keep safely trapped inside. That is what we really reject, because it would make us very vulnerable.

Now I just keep saying, "Your will be done," and he wills to have me for one of his children. There is still human pain, but there is also peace. There is still rejection, but there is also acceptance. I used to think I just had to struggle through this life on earth and then, perhaps, I would be able to go "elsewhere" and live with God. Now I believe that God and I together struggle through my life on earth. We live together now, but its not perfect because I'm not perfect.

But you know what? Even with the defects and shortcomings, limitations and imperfections, life is so much easier and more enjoyable now. I know that God loves me, but how much and in how many different ways I am still learning. I know that God wants me to be whole and complete as he created me, but I am still learning what is missing. I know that God is involved in my life and the life of all he created, but how involved and in what new ways I am still learning.

I thought that improving my conscious contact with God would make God even more real than he had already become, and it did. But even more noticeable than that, it made me more real.

Reflection Questions

1. What happens when you pray to God, 'Your will be done'?

2. What happens at the intersection of your humanity and God's divinity?

3. Does conscious contact with God make you more real? In what ways?

You received without payment, give without payment

(Mt 10:8)

Step Twelve

Having had a spiritual awakening as a result of these steps, we tried to carry this message to alcoholics and practice these principles in all our affairs.

I am a human being who has known the desperate, painful experience of mere "existence" and can assure you that "living" is not only possible but more pleasant. There are no permanent solutions to our temporal problems, but there are temporal solutions that work while we're here. If you can be at peace with the "temporary," it will be enough.

I know that if you are anything like me you cannot look at me now and see yourself if you are still trapped by alcohol or any of the other heartaches of our humanity. When I first met them at the AA meetings, my fellow alcoholics looked and sounded reasonably healthy. When they related the "how it was" part of their stories, however, they entered into my then present condition and I knew they had been there before because their description was so accurate. They allowed me to touch their wounds and, at the same time, I could see they were no longer hurting or needing to withdraw from their experiences. I could see that they remembered how it felt to be broken and desperate and enslaved. But they didn't feel that way now.

Remembering the whole story is a crucial part of staying sober. Over and over again I heard, "Think it through to the end":

It's too easy, when I'm in the midst of pain, to remember the relief I got from anesthetizing myself with alcohol and forget what it was like when I came to.

It's too easy, when I'm struggling with reality, to remember the escape alcohol and my defects provided and forget the insanity I escaped into.

It's too easy to remember, when relationships are dying, how I thought I had control of others when I had only lost control of myself.

It's too easy to rationalize and procrastinate and let my feelings become facts or to look for instant solutions or to shame myself and blame others, and forget that's how I got to the bottom.

Today, I have to learn new things and do hard things because I believe my fellow alcoholics when they say, "We thought we could find an easier, softer way, but we could not." The ways of the world are easy and the road is wide. The ways of AA and God are simple but hard to follow and the path is narrow —just Twelve Steps wide.

Practicing these principles in all my affairs is what I strive for today—with imperfect results. Just knowing the principles does not ensure that they will be applied automatically. It takes conscious effort and subconscious awareness, and many times that happens after the fact because I still act without thinking. I am getting better at it, though, and that is what counts.

Feelings are frequently the culprit because they are strong forces but are not principles. Principles are fundamental truths, and feelings are only symptoms or expressions of opinion or sentiment. Don't get me wrong. I'm not saying we shouldn't have feelings; I'm saying we shouldn't build our house (or reality) on them because they are as changing as the sand. Feelings are useful tools when properly used as signals or symptoms. They can lead me to search for the proper principle if I let them.

I believe that is a great deal of the help my sponsor gave me when she made me write both sides of my inventory. The fundamental truth that came out was that nothing is *all* good or *all* bad. I felt bad, ashamed, defeated, "no good," but that did not mean that I was only bad, shameful, hopeless, and had no good in me. My feelings were symptoms of the kind of life I had been leading and the choices I had made, but I was not limited to that.

So maybe that's my invitation to you in this Twelfth Step: Don't be limited to your feelings. On the other side, don't protect yourself from taking an honest look at who you are just to avoid having those "bad" feelings. Find someone who can help you look at not only the visible, human limitations on the outside but also the hidden good on the inside.

Nothing changed for me when I spent my time dwelling on those who didn't seem to love or want me. It changed when I found some people who did. Nothing changed when I thought I had to find all the answers myself, because I never found them all and so I was stuck with what I already knew. Nothing changed when I spent my time groaning that I deserved more than I had. It changed when I became grateful that I have what I need.

Today, I am sure I have far more than I deserve, but it is a gift and gifts have nothing to do with merit or worthiness or badness or goodness or status or power. God doesn't love me and care for me because I'm worth it or have earned his love. He loves me because he is God. That is what God does. For me that is a fundamental truth.

That is the message I try to carry today. Help is available. Change is possible. What seems lost today can be found. Salvation is promised and can be obtained—if we want it and are willing to go to any lengths to get it.

Reflection Questions

1. What is your life like when you "think it through to the end"?

2. Do your feelings lead you toward or away from your principles?

3. God loves you because he is God. That is what God does. What does that mean for your life?

Trees planted by streams of water . . .

(Ps 1:1-3)

I define "spirit" as that which is inside of me that motivates me to do what I do and be who I am. For many years, my motivation came predominantly from my own human spirit—my own ego. I went to church, had deep convictions about God's presence in the world, and still wound up drinking as a "solution" to life's trials and tribulations. It is obvious to me now that I did not know how to apply my knowledge and beliefs.

The Twelve Step program of Alcoholics Anonymous, which is a spiritual program, allowed me to personally experience what had previously only been "head stuffing." Having knowledge about God is not the same as having an experience of God. Today, I am reminded of a complaint registered by my oldest son regarding his twelve-plus years of Catholic education: "They teach you all of this information but don't teach you how to use it."

Looking back over some of the Scriptures, I can see that Jesus didn't just teach "facts," he shared human and divine experiences through his parables. He lived with his disciples, sharing their lifestyle and introducing them to new possibilities. We all need the activities and events through which knowledge is gained and an environment that invites us to live out that knowledge. We all need to experience the sharing so we can share the experience.

AA provides this "free to learn and live" type of environment. We learn to share ourselves, not just words. We learn to go beyond our right to be diverse and share our broken humanity, which helps us find what we have in common. We learn to appreciate our need for each other as a strength rather than denying our need for help for fear that we will appear weak.

I can still remember a meeting where a young man was sharing a spiritual experience he had and seemed genuinely surprised that what he had done worked. He said, "You know, I've read the Bible, gone to church, read these Twelve Steps, and come to meetings for over a year, and it never occurred to me to take any of it seriously and personally." When he did, he saw all that is promised happen in his own life.

The Twelve Steps are written in the plural—we, our, us. The "I" stories that I share let me know I'm part of the "we" and remind me what we all have in common. If I don't take the Twelve Steps seriously and personally, my "I" story will remain in the "what was" and the "what is" categories and I will not experience the miracle of "what can be." I used to see life as a jigsaw puzzle where I had to try to get all the pieces to fit so I could see the picture. Now I believe it's more like a crossword puzzle—the definition is given but what you write in the spaces has to be right both horizontally and vertically or it doesn't work.

There's another saying in AA: "The AA program isn't for those who need it; it's for those who want it." There are many alcoholics who are still suffering because they aren't able to "want it" yet.

The world I live in today isn't filled only with suffering alcoholics who are seeking help. There are many people in our society who are looking for a way to change their lives, to find a purpose and meaning for their being, to discover where and to whom they belong.

We all need support from each other and a "safe" place to grow and change, to make peace with our daily problems, a Higher Power, ourselves, and each other, because a "spiritual" way of life is not necessarily the popular thing in our culture today.

I hope my vision that more and more of us want a spiritual life is true because I believe that God, as I understand him, still weeps over his people—not because we are bad, but because we are in pain. He no doubt has the biggest heartache of all because he is powerless over us unless we give him permission to actively enter our lives and heal us. Then we will see the strength and growth, the ability to withstand both the winters and summers of life, the glory and the humility of our humanity. We can live in confidence that we will receive all the nourishment we need—like trees planted by streams of water.

MORE BOOKS FOR SPIRITUAL RECOVERY AND PRAYER

Take and Make Holy: Honoring the Sacred in the Healing Journey of Abuse Survivors
by Mari West Zimmerman
Prayer services honoring the mystery of God's presence in a survivor's experience of healing. They follow approximately the sequence of milestones in the recovery process. Meant to accompany, not replace, professional therapy. Important for abuse survivors, counselors, therapists, spiritual directors and pastors. 198 pages. ISBN 1-56854-094-9

A Reconciliation Sourcebook
edited by Kathleen Hughes and Joseph A. Favazza
A wide range of texts about alienation and reconciliation from many cultural and disciplinary perspectives. Built around the parable of the Prodigal Son, these texts explore ten themes, from division and alienation through penance, mercy and celebration. 212 pages. ISBN 1-56854-098-1

I Will Lie Down This Night
by Melissa Musick Nussbaum
A mother and master storyteller shares vignettes of and reflections on her family's bedtime rituals and nighttime prayers. Reawaken the anticipation, the resolution and the vulnerability that the dark end of the day used to call to mind before we "grew up." Includes texts of many traditional night prayers. 152 pages. ISBN 1-56854-085-X

I Will Arise This Day
by Melissa Musick Nussbaum
A delightful little book filled with anecdotes, prayers and reflections about morning prayer, supported by sound theology and earthy spirituality. The appendix includes psalms and other texts for morning prayer. 154 pages. ISBN 1-56854-135-X

The Psalter
The ICEL translation of the 150 psalms in a prayer or study book. A wonderful gift for those searching for a way to pray, a way to walk the path that has sustained synagogue and church throughout the centuries. 392 pages. ISBN 0-929650-77-8

Order from your Bookstore or from
Liturgy Training Publications.